Best Wishes
Mirrie Cardew

# A BASENJI FOR ME

A BASENJI FOR ME . . because . . . .

*He is unique.*

*He is different.*

*He does not bark.*

*He is exceptionally clean.*

*He has meticulous habits.*

*He lacks doggy smell.*

*He washes himself like a cat.*

*He yodells when pleased.*

*He is an excellent house dog.*

*He makes an ideal family pet, companion and friend.*

*He is a handy size*

*He is hardy and sporting.*

*He loves you when you are down.*

*He celebrates when you are up.*

*He enjoys a good walk and romp and equally*
*enjoys sharing your fireside, your home,your heart.*

*The illustration opposite is reproduced from an original pastel drawing by Doriene McQueen.*

# A Basenji for Me

MIRRIE CARDEW

## PREFACE

It is now six years since the first edition of 'A Basenji for Me' and the little book seems to be still much in demand. It is meant to be a handbook for anyone wanting information about this delightfully clever and fascinating breed.

Our much beloved old *Champion Falcon* along with a few of his offspring have gone to 'the happy hunting ground' — they gave us much pleasure.

I had a Basenji as a pet some years before I married, and I gave Tony a beautiful red Basenji puppy *(Crackertwo of the Congo)* as a wedding present. I bought *Crackertwo* from Mrs Veronica Tudor-Williams, who kindly gave me his mother *Kasui of the Congo* to keep him company. *Kasui* was bred from two of the original imports. Our five sons were brought up with the breed as well as many other pets. We lived in a large house and I look back on those years with much happiness. Tony and I now live in a small cottage, and Tony is chairman of the Basenji Breed Council which incorporates the three breed clubs.

We still have a single bitch who this year has had a glorious litter of five, to Miss Tudor-Williams Australian and English Champion *Afrika Royal Challenge of the Congo* (an imported dog). Maybe I shall be tempted to show one of the puppies along with my Chinese Crested — who are identical in character to Basenjis.

This year Tony and I celebrate our 40th wedding anniversary, so you see, we have shared much of our life with the breed — and 'A Basenji' is still a much loved dog 'For Me'.

*Mirrie Cardew*
March 1986

*The photograph on the opposite page was taken in 1950 and features the author and 'Crackertwo of the Congo'.*

ISBN 0 904597 65 2 Printed in England

Published by Midland Counties Publications
24 The Hollow, Earl Shilton, Leicester, LE9 7NA, UK.

CONTENTS

## A SHORT HISTORY OF THE BREED

This delightful breed of dog has possibly been with man since time immemorial. He is said to have originated in darkest Africa where the Central African tribes use him as a hunting dog, to scent out game and to follow wounded animals. The natives fasten primative bells made from gourds or hollowed out wood so they can hear the dogs when hidden in the long grasses. Although Basenjis do not bark, they do make all the other doggy noises.

Dr. Schweinfurth,who travelled in Africa in the late 1860s wrote in his book 'The Heart of Africa' a great deal about the dogs of the various tribes. Describing the Niam-Niam tribe (pronounced 'yum-yum') he wrote 'The only domesticated animals are poultry and dogs; the dogs belong to a small breed resembling the wolf dog, but with short sleek hair. They have ears that are always erect: and a short curly tail like a pig, and are usually a bright yellowish tan colour with a white stripe on the neck'.

It is possible the breed spread to Egypt, as the breed we know today so very much resembles the dogs depicted on the ancient tombs: often sitting at the feet of the Pharoah kings. This breed has also been written about by the late Dr. Paul Schiebestain in 'My Pygmy and Negro Hosts' and in Martin Johnson's Congorilla'.

The dogs have always been highly prized by their native owners, and used to be regarded more highly than a wife because they relied upon their dog to find food.

Basenji-like dogs were exhibited as 'African Bush Dogs' (often known as 'Congo Terriers') at Crufts dog show in 1895. Dr. W. R. Temple bought the pair but they died soon afterwards from a virus infection. It was said that another pair were exhibited in Paris about the same time.

The Lady Helen Nutting brought six of these dogs back from Bahr-el-Ghazal (on the borders of the Congo) in 1923, and during quarantine they also died following experimental distemper innoculations.

So we have to thank Mrs Olivia Burn and her 1936/37 imports for the foundation of the lovely breed we know today, and also Miss Veronica Tudor-Williams, who later imported a number of dogs (including the now famous 'Fula of The Congo') and who also kept the breed going during the war years with much care and cost when it could have so easily disappeared again.

We are indeed so lucky that Mrs Burn had such an excellent eye for a dog, being a well known owner of 'The Blean' wire fox terriers in England. It was while she was staying with her husband in the Belgian Congo, that she saw this distinct breed, all so very true to type. She was able to choose her foundation stock from those bred by Tribal chiefs in the interior and the dogs had to travel many hundreds of miles by river steamer and train before being flown back to England. The dogs soon grew heavier coats to compensate for the English winter climate and survived quarantine successfully.

The dogs were passed as a pure breed by the Kennel Club and zoological experts and were duly registered at The Kennel Club under the breed 'Basenji', said to be a translation of 'Bush thing' or 'Little thing of the bush', in the hound group.

Mrs Burn's original imports 1936-1937 included: *Bongo of Blean, Bokoto of Blean, Bashele of Blean, Bereke of Blean, Bungwa of Blean and Bakuma of Blean. Bongo* and *Bokoto* were among the first Basenjis exhibited at the 1937 Crufts Dog show and were said to have caused quite a sensation, requiring police control of the crowds who had come to see the dogs who did not bark. *Bakuma* was exported later to the U.S.A.

Miss Tudor-William's imported dogs included; *Simolo of The Congo, Wau of The Congo and Fula of The Congo.*

Mr and Mrs Arthur Byron brought back from the Sudan a little dog called *Amatangazig*, who later became *Amatangazig of The Congo* when she went to Miss Tudor-Williams during the war; and was to become a valuable acquisition to the breed.

Most of the present-day Basenjis in the western world are bred from the original 'Blean' and 'of The

Congo' stock. Additional imported blood came from a little stowaway Basenji who arrived in Boston from West Africa in the 'forties. Rescued by Mr Alexander Phemister, 'Congo' as she was called was mated to his 'Phemisters Bois' who had previously been registered in the U.K. as 'Bakuma of Blean'.

Another pair of native Basenjis arrived with a shipment of gorillas and other animals from Africa to New York in 1941 for Mr Teffich of New York. They were called 'Kindu' and 'Kaysenji'. A son from this pair, bred in America, became American Champion Kingolo, and this was later imported into Ireland by Mr and Mrs R. J. Williams, proving a valuable outcross and in most of the Basenji pedigrees today.

Miss Tudor-William's exports in 1940 to a Dr. Richmond in Canada were the foundation of most of the Basenjis in Canada and the States with the addition of the previous-mentioned imports to U.S.A.

Mrs Elspeth Ford of the well known 'Taysenji' prefix, brought back the first black and white Champion Basenji to England from Zambia. The dog 'Champion Taysenji Tahzu' won his title before he came to the U.K. having been shown under South African Kennel Club Rules.

The Basenji Club of Great Britain was formed by the original band of enthusiasts in 1939, the aims of the club being: 'to keep the native ideal, and yet to show the western world what a facinating dog the Basenji is'.

The Basenji Club of America was formed and the first Basenjis were shown at The Westminster Kennel Club show (our equivalent to Crufts) in 1945.

A charming story in the U.S.A.'s 'Saturday Evening Post' (at that time a famous pictorial weekly with a terrific circulation) titled 'Weep no more my Lady' was written by the well known author James Street, and this became the novel 'Goodbye my Lady'. This was then made into a feature film of the same name by Warner Brothers and did much to publicise the breed. I believe the original story was inspired and

*Champion St. Erme Dancing Eagle*

written around Mr George Gilkey's bitch 'Tanya of Windrush' bred from the first Basenjis exported to Canada by Miss Tudor-William's; Tanyas painting being used as an illustration by the Evening Post.

Another Basenji, 'My Lady of The Congo' was imported from England into the U.S.A. to star in that film and the then boy star, Brandon de Wilde, played the leading role. The film won an award and was acclaimed world-wide putting the breed firmly on the map. The film was later bought by our own B.B.C. and always causes much interest when screened.

The Basenji is an exceptionally healthy and hardy dog. Sporting, intelligent, faithful and exceptionally clean in his ways. Although he does not bark he can almost talk with a variety of lovely sounds and the most unique yodel - a gift he uses to greet his owner and when he is most happy and excited.

Although originating from a hot country, he enjoys the snow but hates the rain. If he does get wet he will lick himself dry like a cat. One of the earliest published captions above a photograph of Basenjis in

*Suzie's Friend (Pippin)*

*'Falcon' and Nicholas 1966-77. Britain's top winning Basenji (29CCs) Ch. St. Erme Fula Falcon of the Congo, with Nicholas Cardew, Rutland, 1966 and 1977.*

a pre-war *Tatler* read: 'Take one when you buy a flat - half an angel, half a cat'. I have always felt this a very apt description.

The Basenji makes an ideal pet and to many, the perfect family dog. He will adore the youngest of the children, play and romp with the older ones, be happy going out shopping, trekking in the countryside, staying home by the fireside and perhaps best of all - sharing your armchair if you are lonely and need companionship. Although he cannot bark he is an excellent house dog and guard, and will give warning when anyone approaches your home night or day. He is an upstanding, smart smooth coated animal of handy size and with his alert expression, slanting eyes and puzzled frown, clean limbs and curly tail, he is what he looks, a real thoroughbred.

Several Basenjis in Great Britain have been trained to the gun and some have done well in obedience.

He comes in three colour variations, Chestnut, Pure Black and Black & Tan — all with white points. Varying from a full white collar, full white waistcoat, stockings and blaze, to just a little white on his feet but always a white shirt front and a white tip to his very curly tail (which ought to lie flat to one side or the other, of his body). He is an ideal size small enough to tuck under ones arm, yet tough enough to walk for miles if his owner so wishes. He is exceptionally adaptable and only too happy to fit in with the moods and whims of his owner.

## CHOOSING A PUPPY

Basenjis are almost all in pet homes with owners who dote on their dogs and once a Basenji owner always a Basenji owner or so it seems. So if you think a Basenji is for you I recommend a visit to one of the larger dog shows. Basenjis are scheduled at most of the important shows and these are usually widely advertised. Seek out the Basenji benches and chat up the owners who are always more than ready to talk

*Puppies by Ch. Falcon, Ex St. Erme Susan Pony.*

about their pets. Ask if they have any litters planned and, with luck, you may get on their waiting list. Basenjis, unlike other breeds, only breed once a year and almost always in the winter. Very few puppies are born in the summer even though the breed has now been established in Britain for so many years. We invite our would be puppy owners to come and see the babies in the nest. Much as one would like to keep them all, this is not always possible. So it is rather fun to choose the puppy for the right owner. Many people say a bitch makes the nicer pet. For many years I believed this but now I consider the dogs are a little more independent, and have a little more character. But maybe I am prejudiced owning one of the most delightful male Basenjis — the great and famous Champion St. Erme Fula Falcon of the Congo, now is his 14th year.

However, whether you choose a dog or bitch try and visit the breeder and ask to see the parents and, better still, the grandparents if possible. I always say 'Show me the grandparents and I will know what the puppies will be like when adult'. It is usual for a puppy to go to his new home at 12 weeks; by this time he ought to have been vaccinated by a veterinary surgeon and be safe to take out.

A new puppy is a new responsibility, a new friend to be part of the family. His happiness and health is in your hands now. Vaccinations are most sophisticated and give maximum immunity against such virus infections as distemper, hardpad, hepititus, leptospirosis, canocola and parvo-virus.

*Potential Champions: Left - Dancing Eagle at six weeks. Right - A red/white and tricolour litter by Ch. Falcon, Ex St. Erme Dolly Pony.*

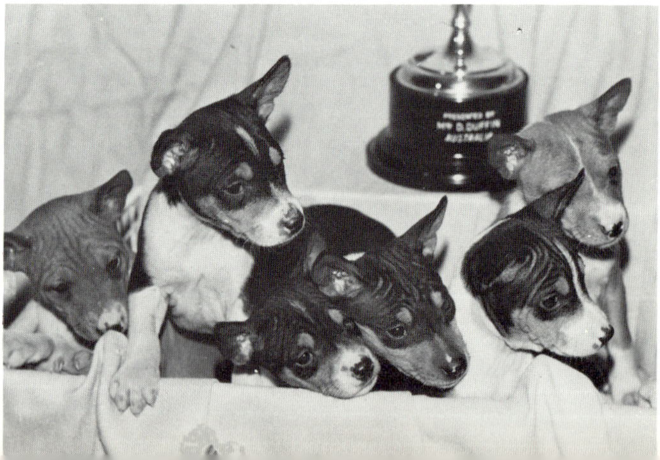

*St. Erme Pony Pageant.*

## FEEDING A PUPPY

When you take him home he ought also to be fully weaned and eating three meals a day. It is usual for the breeder to supply a diet sheet so that you can make as little change as possible in his daily routine. Our 12 week old puppies have approximately half a pint of warm milk, at 8 a.m. with porridge, cornflakes or baby cereal, plus a small handful of puppy biscuits to play with and keep him amused. At noon he has 4 ozs of fresh or cooked meat with a cupful of scalded puppy or terrier meal, plus his vitamin tablets and a little grated carrot, greens or onion. Tea time: he has another half pint of milk with a scrambled or boiled egg plus a handful of baby rusks or 'All-in-One' dog food of which there are several on the market today. Many like 'Purina' and 'Spratts' high protein feeds are fine on their own but fresh clean water must always be available especially when feeding the dry foods.

Our puppies and adults always have safe knuckle bones to chew. Far better a puppy does his chewing on a bone than your best slippers chewing keeps him happy and occupied, is good for his teeth and gums and is a rich source of nourishment into the bargain.

Get your puppy accustomed to different tastes. Fish, chicken, rabbit and hare are very nutritious, but do take care never to give him bones from these. I find a microwave oven ideal for cooking dog meat.

You will find your local pet shop a treasure house of pet foods and accessories. Nine million households in Britain have pets, so pet food is big business and much thought and care is put into producing it. Most of the recognised brands of food will be alright for your dog but if you are lucky to have a good butcher who can sell you fresh meat and offal, (such as tripe and hearts) and safe marrow bones, your Basenji will indeed be in clover.

An adult Basenji needs one good nourishing meal a day plus a snack.

*Staying put! Puppies by Ch. Dancing Eagle Ex St. Erme Dancing Faun.*

## TRAINING YOUR PUPPY

We assume your puppy has been fully vaccinated and wormed so you can now get him used to a soft leather collar. If you have a garden take your puppy out as soon as he has had his food. You will have the odd accident but Basenjis are very easy to train and will soon realise he has to go outside to make his pools, etc. A cardboard box lined with newspaper and a small blanket or towel will be a perfect bed for him; especially if it can be put in a warm corner of the kitchen. A bone will keep him happy and amused the first few nights as he is sure to miss his litter mates. If you succomb and take him upstairs he will expect to go up every night. It's the old rule: once allowed, always allowed; once forbidden always forbidden. It's not fair to allow him on the best sofa one day and smack him the next. So give him his own corner from the start and make a fuss of him when he is extra good.

When you eventually introduce him to a lead he will at least have got used to his collar. One of the best ways to train a puppy to walk is to take him to a quiet spot, speak gently to him and encourage him to follow you on the lead. An important DON'T: do not pull or yank the lead as this can put the puppy off walks for some time. If, however, you make the lesson short and enjoyable, moving off at a brisk pace, speaking encouraging words, giving a tit bit as he gets the message right he will soon trot along happily. Many people find an older dog most helpful as the puppy will try and follow suit. Another method is to follow the puppy around in the direction he is going until he gets used to the lead. Above all patience is a great virtue. If you are both a trifle exasperated give up and try again later. Most puppies are happier playing loose in the garden and I have to admit some of my best show dogs went on a lead for the first time only a day or two before their first show. Training proper can begin at about 4 months. If you live in a town the local canine society will put you in touch with the local dog training classes. The classes range from simple obedience for family pets to ring craft. These can be fun and beneficial to owner and dog because your dog is taught to sit, heel and stay — useful lessons to know if your Basenji is going to have the pleasure of running loose in the park later and you want him quickly. One also meets other owners, exchange experiences, your pet gets used to

*St. Erme Dancing Mischief and St. Erme Floral Dance at eight weeks.*

other dogs and that too is an advantage when you take him to a show.

Although most pet owners just seek a companion, remember you are going to feed and care for your pet for possibly ten years or more. So it is to your advantage to have a smart, sweet-natured pet in blooming health. Never take a runt nor a puppy with some defect — it will be a constant worry even if you feel sorry for him. Thank goodness most breeders wish to keep their reputation and will no doubt encourage you to show the puppy. A full grown Basenji living in a town will be happy with two outings a day, preferably where he can have a good free run. He can then be left to play happily around the house and garden. If the weather is good your pet will prefer to be out most of the time, but if it is windy cold or damp, he will be only too happy to rush outdoors to complete his toilet and nip back indoors, as quick as he can, to a warm spot.

A much loved family Basenji is usually in pretty good show fettle. If he is stroked and patted and has a scupulously clean sleeping quarter he will seldom need bathing, or grooming as such. In spring, an adult Basenji grows a new coat so it is a good idea to brush him daily so as to rid his coat of dead hair. Dogs kept in kennels tend to grow heavier coats in winter and it takes quite a time to get them back into sparkling coat. The house pet has a definite advantage over the kennel dog. Basenjis do not care for kennel life much, they love human companionship and are much less trouble if their welfare is pandered to.

## FIRST AID

Apart from virus infections (which are now covered by the excellent vaccines) and barring accidents, your pet ought to be set for a long and healthy life. Should your pet be involved in an accident make

"Sit"

sure he is put in a quiet place as quickly as possible. It is useful to have a sedative from your vet in your first-aid box and a bottle of T.C.P. for stings and scratches. Eye lotion will aid getting a speck of dust from his eye. If he should get bitten by another dog it is best to get him a penicillin injection from the vet as quickly as possible since this can prevent a serious abcess and complications later on. A torn ear can be held between two sterile bits of lint on which a few grains of permanganate of potash have been sprinkled. A puppy that may have swallowed poison can be tempted to take a little milk before you get him and (if possible) a sample of the poison as quickly as you çan to your vet. A broken or suspected fracture calls for quick action. A Vet is your and your dog's best friend; prevention is better than cure and usually much cheaper.

St. Erme Dancing Faun - a typical show/breed Basenji.

## BREEDING

A Basenji bitch usually comes into season at about eleven months to a year old (one of the joys of this breed) but if you do not wish to breed, a hormone pill is available from your vet. I have had my bitches on the pill with much success, usually giving the pill before an expected heat. The bitches have had no side effects whatsoever and gone are the worries of being afraid to let them out with male dogs. One bitch I had on the pill for two years running. She then came into season the following year, was mated and produced a fine litter of six. If you decide to breed a litter of puppies it is considered better to wait until the bitch is fully mature, say about 2 years, her second season; although year old Basenjis are quite capable of being excellent mothers. However, I think a bitch that has left puppyhood behind is really more ideal as a mother. You will naturally have thought of a suitable stud dog and perhaps the breeder of your puppy is the best person to consult as she will know the characters and traits in her own stock. If you can manage to take your Basenji to a top show dog with good temperament as well as heritage, then you ought. A beautiful animal however near perfection is no earthly good as a show dog unless he has a lovely outgoing nature to match, and a top show winner usually has that little extra personality that has taken him to the top in the first place.

It is usual to take the bitch to the dog for mating from the 12th to 15th day. If you take her too early on in her heat, although the dog may be keen on her, she will more than likely be exceptionally rude to the dog; even trying to bite him. The stud dogs owner will not be very pleased either as her dog once scenting your bitch is going to feel very frustrated and unsettled. With reasonable luck they will mate around the 13th day, tie probably for about 20 minutes, and then you can take her home.

## TAKING CARE OF THE IN-WHELP BITCH

You will discover that once she has been mated, her season will shortly be over. However, do not let her loose with other dogs for another two weeks just to be on the safe side. Now is the time to check if she is due for any Booster vaccinations. Better to see she has full immunity to pass on to her unborn offspring. Your Vet may suggest worming her again although it is usual practice now to worm ones dogs regularly for both round worm and tape worm. It is possible to buy preparations from your pet shop but often cheaper and more satisfactory to aquire any drugs from the vet. Let your bitch lead as normal a life as possible for the first month. You then ought to see a definite thickening around her middle, especially after a big meal. You could give her extra protein in the way of meat, eggs and fish but do not feed her late at night unless you want her to get you up.

Now is the time to provide her with a suitable box in which to have her puppies. I suggest a wooden box, approximately 1 metre square — preferably with a hinged lid and a board across the open front to keep out draughts and keep bedding in. Put it in a warm quiet corner and let her get used to sleeping in the box at least 3 weeks before her litter is due.

## WHELPING

It is normal for a bitch to carry her young for sixty-three days. A large litter of seven may arrive a few days early and an odd puppy be up to three days late. As long as your Basenji is content do not over fuss her. She can go out for short walks, but if you have a garden I suggest she is allowed to 'potter about' at her own discretion. Basenjis are easy whelpers and excellent mothers. Shelf paper or clean newspapers make ideal bedding. Your Basenji will do much scratching and tearing up of the paper to make a nest, indicating her puppies early arrival. She may go off her food but Basenjis often eat very well just before whelping, as if preparing for a 'long lie-in'. She may scratch and pant before actually straining (in labour proper) and although she may make a fuss just before the first puppy arrives, she will then settle down with little or no problems.

Once she really begins to stretch and push, often accompanied by little cries and grunts the first puppy will soon arrive — usually head first and enclosed in its own water sack. Do not interfere, as the mother knows exactly what to do and will sever the umbilical cord, clean up the afterbirth (placenta), and proceed to wash her puppy vigourously. It will be suckling within moments of birth. Other puppies usually arrive at hourly intervals, but do not worry if the gap is longer. Sometimes a mother will go off to sleep for a couple of hours and as her pushing pains start again

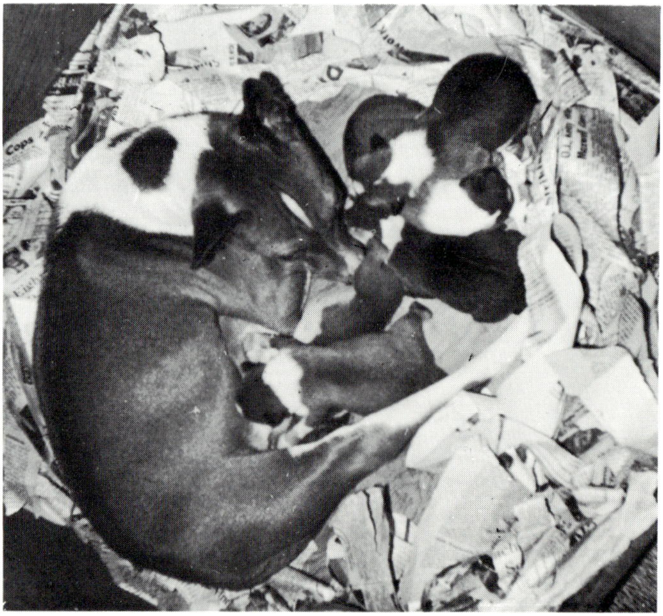

*New-born puppies.*

will then have the rest of her puppies fairly quickly.

When you think she has finished, you can offer her a drink of warm milk laced with glucose. She ought now to settle down for several hours.

If by any chance she does not settle — the chances are she may still have another puppy inside her or, if she actually strains and pushes for two hours without sign of a puppy do not hesitate to consult your Vet — who ought to have been put in the picture about your expected litter, in any case.

I would stress that Basenjis are one of the easiest animals to breed. One just needs to make sure she has a suitable warm place to call her own and a little moral support from her doting owner in the early stages.

## TAKING CARE OF THE PUPPIES

Basenjis usually have an excellent supply of milk. Enabling them to feed even a large litter for at least seven weeks and often longer. You will find the mother will only leave her offspring for a few moments for the first week, although she will stay away a little longer as they grow older. It is advisable to have the puppies dew claws removed by your veterinary surgeon on the 3rd day.

The mother will need two good nourishing meals plus two milky snacks a day. You can offer the puppies a little baby cereal in warm milk from four weeks. Start by dipping their noses in the dish gently, and by the second day they will be lapping. A little scraped meat will also be much appreciated.

From six weeks of age, the puppy might be eating as follows: 8A.M. — Baby Cereal or Weetabix with warm full cream cows milk, to which I add 1 egg yolk for every two puppies and crushed Can-o-vel vitamin tablets. NOON — First size puppy meal (scalded with hot water or gravy) with 1½ ozs (per puppy) of fresh minced meat or high quality tinned dog meat. 4 P.M. — SCRAMBLED EGG (1 egg between 2 puppies) or milk rice sago semolina pudding or one of the 'complete puppy foods' i.e. 'Purina', 'Pedigree Pup' etc. Also a drink of warm milk. 8 P.M. — The same as 8 a.m.

Cut down to three meals at three months and two meals at six months of age. By the time the puppies are six weeks old it is a good idea to advertise them in the dog journals to find suitable homes. Make sure they are properly weaned, wormed (for round worms at five and seven weeks) and vaccinated by the time they are ready to leave home at approximately 10 to 12 weeks.

## SHOWING

Your Basenji must be registered with the Kennel Club and duly transferred into your name.

Basenjis are quite the easiest of dogs to show. Top class health condition means top class show condition. Providing he can walk on a collar and lead, is sweet natured with his fellow beings and has no real outstanding glaring fault, there is no reason why you should not enter him for exhibition.

*Below left; Ch. Falcon, at one year; Below right: Ch. St. Erme Painted Hawk, (owner Mr & Mrs Alan Bastion).*

*Posing for the Judge at the Brent Open Show.*

In Great Britain there are numerous dogs shows every week run under Kennel Club rules and regulations. These are advertised well in advance in the two weekly dog journals 'Our Dogs' and 'Dog World', also in 'The Kennel Gazette' the official monthly journal of the Kennel Club.

Dog shows fall roughly into three sections. Local dog clubs run 'Sanction' and 'Limited' unbenched shows: Champions cannot be entered for these shows and they are run for the benefit of club members.

Open Shows are open to all dogs from any part of the country. Many open shows are run in conjunction with the many big Agricultural Shows, so they can offer an interesting day out for all the family. These shows are usually benched and many have classes just for Basenjis — ideal for taking out your puppy and meeting fellow enthusiasts.

Championship Shows (of which Crufts is the most famous) are those at which a big variety of breeds are scheduled and the majority of breeds can compete for the much highly prized Kennel Club Challenge Certificates — commonly known among dog folk as 'C.C.'s'. One is offered to the best of each sex in a breed. To add the coveted 'Champion' in front of a

*Above left: Ch. Falcon with owner and the world famous judge, the late Fred Cross, Esq., after winning Leicester Championship Show. Right; U.S.A. Ch. Khajahs Gay Amaryllis with Mrs Shirley Chambers.*

dogs name the dog has to win three challenge certificates under three different judges.

However, C.C.'s are very few and far between when one thinks there can be as many as fifty or more Basenjis at one of the big shows.

The championship shows are always benched and it can be a very long and tiring day to both exhibit and exhibitor, especially if much travelling is involved (to say nothing of the expense).

After a show, it is usual for the judge to write a report on the prize-winners. This is published in the 'Doggy' press. Often one gets an idea of the virtues and faults worthy of note.

If I were to take a young Basenji to a small show I would do the following:

Find a suitable small show being held in my own County. Enter the puppy in suitable puppy classes, for instance: Minor Puppy Dog — 6 to 9 months; Puppy Dog under 12 months; Maiden Dog (a dog that has not won a 1st Prize); and possibly an 'Any Variety Hound Novice' class.

I would see that my puppy was as fit and healthy as possible and take along a few small tit-bits (such as a little chopped chicken or liver). I would also take a small face cloth which I could dampen at the show, to clean his white feet and ensure he goes into the ring immaculate.

*U.S.A. Ch. St Erme Black Dollybird (black/white), owned by Mrs. Earl Evans.*

*Head study of Ch. Falcon. (photo by Les Stone).*

You will be allocated a number which you must fasten or pin on to your suit or dress. If your puppy walks well on his collar and lead, then exhibit on this. One can buy smart white show collars and leads but they are a trifle frail for everyday use. The judge may ask you to put your puppy on a table for close examination of his teeth, coat etc.

You would then be asked to briskly walk your Basenji up the ring and back twice, so that the judge can assess movement and confirmation. When the judge makes the final inspection, you will be expected to have your dog looking as still as possible. This is sometimes where a tit-bit in your hand may persuade your puppy to look alert and animated.

If you are lucky you may come away with a prize. But remember there is an old saying 'Every Champion has at least five faults and the perfect dog has yet to be born', and also, human beings being what they are, each has a different eye and one dog that pleases one judge may not please another.

Once bitten by the 'show bug' your life can be full of endless entertainment. You make many friends

*U.S.A. Ch. Tippisea Sir George with Earl Evans (a Hodges & Associates photo).*

*U.S.A. Ch. Riviana Sea Hawk (owner Mrs Ringle) at the BCDA Eastern Speciality, Buffalo, N.Y.*

and need never be lonely. The dogs have no class distinction — one is on equal terms with everyone else. If you have a real star of a dog that means not only one that fits the standard but one with 'personality plus' — then indeed you will enjoy your Basenji all his days whether he is shown or not.

## SOME DO'S & DON'TS

Do get a licence from the Post Office, when your puppy is 6 months.

Do love your Basenji at all times.

Do provide him with an interesting safe bone if you have to leave him, whilst in early puppyhood.

Do praise him when he makes a real effort to please you.

Do scold him if he is really naughty (tone of voice — far more effective than smacks) being banished from your company. Often does more good than a smack.

Do be sensible about feeding times. A dog is a creature of habit.

Do teach him to spend a little time on his own — right from the start.

Do remember he is one of the cleverest dogs on earth. *You cannot brain-wash him, but you can negotiate with him.*

Do ensure he has a little free exercise each day, if only in the garden.

Do remember if you go to a dog show — it is meant to be enjoyed.

Do be a good sport.

Do not allow him to rush out of doors. The moment you go out teach him to sit and wait for you to say 'go'. This is a useful lesson for town pets.

Do not leave him alone for hours. Basenjis love company, even if it is only the family cat or tortoise!

Do not let him leap up at all and everyone. Some of your friends may treasure their clothes.

Do not let him foul the footpaths — teach him to use the gutter in towns, hedge rows in the countryside.

Do not encourage him to be naughty with other dogs. Dogs allowed off the lead to romp in the park — usually play and are the best of pals. Dogs on leads usually want to guard their owners when they meet other dogs.

Do not over-feed your puppy late at night and not expect him to have accidents on the kitchen floor.

Do not give old clothes and shoes to chew. It is difficult for him to know the difference between your garden outfit and your best outfit.

Do not push the responsibility of your pet on to others. He is yours and if you really love him, he will own you always

## QUESTIONS AND ANSWERS

*Ought I to insure my Basenji?*
Yes, you are legally responsible for any accident your dog may cause. It is possible to insure your dog through your own household policy for third party. However I recommend you to take out a complete policy to cover third party, death by accident, illness or disease, loss by stealing or straying, veterinary fees or loss of value. Additional insurance can cover animals sent abroad or bitches in whelp. Many breeders of valuable dogs give a free months insurance with each puppy sold, and suggests the new owner keeps the policy up.

*My puppy is car sick, what do I do?*
Do not feed before a journey. Give instead a spoonful of glucose in a little water.

*Do you recommend my taking my dog in the car?*
Basenjis usually enjoy car rides. Do if possible have a guard, and never allow your pet on the front seats.

*If my puppy chews things when I leave him alone what do I do?*
Make sure he has been fed and excercised before you go out. Provide him with a comfortable bed and a good safe bone. Do not leave any dog alone for too long, he will only become sad and frustrated.

*Will my Basenji pine for me if I leave him in boarding kennels?*
More than likely, ask the kennel owner to find a small friendly dog for him to share his kennel with. Two dogs are far easier to leave than one.

*Do I need to bath my Basenji often?*
Hardly ever, perhaps once a year after he has shed his old coat.

*My dog has a violent tummy upset, what do I do?*
If he is otherwise fit and well, rest his tummy and give him the white of one raw egg. If in doubt consult your vet.

*May I change the brand of dog food occasionally?*
Yes! Dogs love variety the same as we do. Remember the top brands have had years of expense and research put into them.

*Is it safe to use weed-killers in the garden?*
My vet says NO. Many weed-killers are dangerous to dogs, one in particular has no known antidote.

*My Basenji is rather fat and does not eat so much. What do you suggest?*
Feed in the morning only, some dogs seem to get fat from sheer contentment.

*Does my Basenji need to wear a coat in the winter?*
No, nature compensates for the winter when your dog grows a heavier coat.

*What do I do if my bitch gets accidentally mated?*
Take veterinary advice at once.

*How often ought I to worm my dog?*
Regularly, your vet will supply tablets for the two common types of worm in dogs.

*Can anyone go to a dog show?*
Yes, for a small entrance fee. You will always find someone to chat to, and no one need ever be lonely whilst dog shows exist.

*Do you think one should keep ones old pet alive as long as possible?*
No, quality of life is all that matters. If your pet no longer enjoys life and is suffering, it is far kinder to have your vet put him to sleep.

*Is it very upsetting?*
No, with modern sophisticated drugs (remember animals get them before humans) your pet will not feel a thing. You will naturally be upset, but your beloved pets feelings ought to come before yours.

*Is it a good idea to have another dog at once?*
This is up to you, but remember no two dogs are alike. Do not expect a successor to be a replica of the other.

*Need I buy the most expensive food for my Basenji?*
No, shop around but as with our own food we pay for expensive packaging; fresh meat and offal is often far cheaper than tinned.

*We are all out at work, is it fair to keep a Basenji?*
No, this breed in particular love companionship, a Basenji on his own can be miserable. If a dog is left for a few hours, he ought at least to have another pet to keep him company. An old Basenji my father-in-law owned would only be happy if the tortoise shared her basket. Having a dog is rather like having a child in the house. Only have a Basenji if you really wish to belong to him for the rest of his days.

# Basenji Photo Album

*Mirrie in 1948 with puppy St Erme Dinka on her lap plus Crackertwo of the Congo (Tristram Shandy) and Kasui of the Congo by her side.*

*'Who says we cannot sit?' St Erme Dancing Faun, Int. Ch. Coral of St Erme (Lakeland Terriers) and Ch. St Erme Dancing Eagle.*

*International & Italian Ch. Arabella Azenda owned by Mrs Margaret Christie-Davies.*

*Old, but much treasured snap of Ch. Falcon 'moving off as a Basenji ought'*

*St. Erme Dancing Finch*

*'You're not going without me'. (Tori at 3 months)*

*Above: Ch. Pukkanut Nocturne —*
*Best-in-Show, Melbourne, Australia, 1978.*
*Owners: Alan & Lauris Hunt.*

*Right: Aust. Ch. Tirhaka Arua Markeeta.*
*Owner Mrs Joan Kay (Australia).*

*Below: Jackie Coulson's Australian*
*Ch. Pharaoh Red Sirocco. Photo: Neilson.*

*Top left: 'Hamish' – Bokoto Nile Foxhunter of Blackpits, recalls success at the Leeds Ch. Show 1985. Photo: McFarlane.*

*Above: St. Erme The Dancing Cat (Ch. Falcon's baby son) with St. Erme Little Wolf, six-month old puppy. Photo: Tony Cardew.*

*Left: Ch. St. Erme Floral Dance, owner Mrs Alan Jenkins. Photo by Diane Pearce.*

*Ch. Taysenji Ti Kibuka,*
*owned by Elspeth M. Ford.*
*Photo by Diane Pearce.*

*Ch. Taysenji Kush,*
*owned by Elspeth M. Ford.*

*Ch. Asaris Ti Karu*
*owned by Elspeth M. Ford.*
*Photograph by Diane Pearce.*

*Diana Berry's St Erme Musical Cat, photographed by Diane Pearce.*

*Ch. Hobby Horse of Sin (sire - St Erme Pony Express) owned by Diana Berry and photographed by Diane Pearce.*

# KENNEL CLUB STANDARD FOR THE BASENJI

CHARACTERISTICS — The Basenji does not bark but is not mute; its own special noise is a mixture of a chortle and a yodel. It is remarkable for its cleanliness in every way. The wrinkled forehead, tightly curled tail, and legs carried straight forward with a swift, long, tireless, swinging stride, are typical of the breed.

GENERAL APPEARANCE — The Basenji should be a lightly built, finely boned aristocratic looking animal, high on the leg compared with its length, always poised, alert and intelligent. The wrinkled head, with pricked ears, should be proudly carried on a well-arched neck. The deep brisket should run up into a definite waist and the tail be tightly curled, presenting a picture of a well-balanced dog of gazelle-like grace.

HEAD AND SKULL — The skull should be flat, well-chiselled and of medium width, tapering towards the nose, with a only a slight stop. The distance from the top of the head to the stop is slightly more than from the stop to the tip of the clean-cheeked appearance. Fine and profuse wrinkles should appear on the forehead when the ears are pricked, side wrinkles are desirable but should not be exaggerated into dewlap. Wrinkles are more noticeable in puppies, but, because of lack of shadowing, are not as noticeable in tri-colours. A black nose is greatly desired.

EYES — Dark, almond shaped, obliquely set, far-seeing and rather inscrutable in expression.

EARS — Small, pointed, erect and slightly hooded, of fine texture, set well forward on top of the head; the tip of the ear should be nearer the centre of the skull than the outside base.

MOUTH — The mouth should be level, with scissors bite, the upper teeth slightly over-lapping and touching the lower teeth.

NECK — Strong and of good length, without thickness, well-crested and slightly full at the base of the throat with a graceful curve accentuating the crest. It should be well-set into laid back shoulders so as to give the head a 'lofty' carriage.

FOREQUARTERS — The shoulders must be well laid back, muscular but not loaded. The points of the scapulae should be fairly close at the withers. The elbows should be firmly tucked in against the brisket. When viewed from in front the elbows should be in line with the ribs and the legs should continue in a straight line to the ground giving a narrow front. The forelegs should be straight with fine bone and very long fore-arms. Pasterns should be of good length, straight but flexible.

BODY — Balanced with short, level back. Ribs well sprung, deep and oval. The loin short-coupled and the deep brisket running up into a definite waist.

HINDQUARTERS — Strong and muscular, with hocks well let down, turned neither in nor out, with long second thighs and moderately bent stifles.

FEET — Small, narrow and compact, with deep pads, well-arched toes and short nails.

TAIL — The tail should be high set with the posterior curve of the buttock extending beyond the root of the tail giving a reachy appearance to the hindquarters. The tail curls tightly over the spine and lies closely to the thigh with a single or double curl.

COAT — Short, sleek and close, very fine. Skin very pliant.

COLOUR — Pure bright red, or pure black, or black and tan, all with white feet, chest and tail tips. White legs, white blaze and white collar optional.

SIZE AND WEIGHT — Ideal heights. Dogs 43cm (17") at shoulder; Bitches 40cm (16"); a few cm (an inch) either way should not penalize an otherwise well-balanced specimen. Ideal weights: Dogs 11 Kg (24lbs); Bitches 9½Kg (21lbs).

FAULTS — Coarse, domed or peaked skull. Muzzle too long or too broad. Cheekiness. Mouth over-shot or under-shot. Round or light eyes. Ears too low-set or too large. Wide chest, barrel ribs, shelly brisket. Short in the leg, out at elbows, toeing in. Heavy bone, cow hocks, low-set or straight tail, thin flat open feet. Long or heavy coat. Creams, sables, or any other colours than those defined in the Colour paragraph above should be heavily penalised. Poor temperament.

NOTE — Male animals should have two apparently normal testicles fully descended into the scrotum.

## OFFICIAL STANDARD FOR THE BASENJI, U.S.A.

CHARACTERISTICS — The Basenji should not bark, but is not mute. The wrinkled forehead and the swift, tireless running gait (resembling a racehorse trotting full out) are typical of the breed.

GENERAL APPEARANCE — The Basenji is a small, lightly built, short backed dog, giving the impression of being high on the leg compared to its length. The wrinkled head must be proudly carried, and the whole demeanor should be one of poise and alertness.

HEAD AND SKULL — The skull is flat, well chiseled and of medium width, tapering towards the eyes. The foreface should taper from eye to muzzle and should be shorter than the skull. Muzzle, neither coarse, nor snipy but with ounded cushions. Wrinkles should appear upon the forehead, and be fine and profuse. Side wrinkles are desirable, but should never be exaggerated into dewlap.

NOSE — Black greatly desired. A pinkish tinge should not penalize an otherwise first class specimen, but it should be discouraged in breeding.

EYES — Dark hazel, almond shaped, obliquely set and far seeing.

EARS — Small, pointed and erect, of fine texture, set well forward on top of head.

MOUTH — Teeth must be level with scissors bite.

NECK — Of good length, well crested and slightly full at base of throat. It should be well set into flat, laid back shoulders.

FOREQUARTERS — The chest should be deep and of medium width. The legs straight with clean fine bone, long forearm and well defined sinews. Pasterns should be of good length, straight and flexible.

BODY — The body should be short and the back level. The ribs well sprung, with plenty of heart room, deep brisket, short coupled, and ending in a definite waist.

HINDQUARTERS — Should be strong and muscular, with hocks well let down, turned neither in nor out, with long second thighs.

FEET — Small, narrow and compact, with well-arched toes.

TAIL — Should be set on top and curled tightly over to either side.

COAT — Short and silky. Skin very pliant.

COLOR — Chestnut red (the deeper the better) or pure black, or black and tan, all with white feet, chest and tail tip. White legs, white blaze and white collar optional.

WEIGHT — Bitches 22 pounds approximately. Dogs 24 pounds approximately.

SIZE — Bitches 16 inches and dogs 17 inches from the ground to the top of the shoulder. Bitches 16 inches and dogs 17 inches from the front of the chest to the farthest point of the hindquarters.

FAULTS — Coarse skull or muzzle. Domed or peaked skull. Dewlap. Round eyes. Low set ears. Overshot or undershot mouths. Wide chest. Wide behind. Heavy bone. Creams, shaded or off colors, other than those defined above, should be heavily penalized.

Approved June 8, 1954.

## USEFUL NAMES AND ADDRESSES

*The names and addresses of the following Basenji club Honorary Secretaries will be of interest and great help to you. Many clubs run their own Championship show and publish a newsletter or chronicle.*

**THE BASENJI CLUB OF GREAT BRITAIN**
Mrs Jean Lord, Garden Cottage, Loddington, Leicester, LE7 9XE, England.

**THE BASENJI OWNERS AND BREEDERS ASSOCIATION**
Mrs E. M. Ford, 129 Maidenhead Road, Windsor, Berks, England.

**THE NORTHERN BASENJI SOCIETY**
Mr J.A. Watson, 47 Cliff Pack Avenue, Wakefield, Yorkshire, England.

**THE BASENJI BREED COUNCIL**
Chairman: Mr Tony St. Erme Cardew, Jasmine Cottage, Burton Lane, Billingborough, Lincolnshire, NG34 0QR, England.

**BASENJI CLUB OF AMERICA**
Mrs Lucretia Hewes, 15675 Kata Drive, Elm Grove, Wisconsin 53122, U.S.A.

**HEART OF MINNESOTA BASENJI CLUB**
Sally Wuornos, Route 1, Box 163, North Branch, Minnesota 55056, U.S.A.

**MID-ATLANTIC BASENJI CLUB**
Cathy Cant, 5601 Green Landing Rd, Upper Marlboro, Maryland 20870, U.S.A.

**EVERGREEN BASENJI CLUB**
Melody Russell, 2714 Northeast 110th, Seattle, Washington 98125, U.S.A.

**GREATER CHICAGOLAND BASENJI CLUB**
Pat De Walt, 1065 Apricot St, Hoffman Estates, Illinois 60195, U.S.A.

**YANKEE BASENJI CLUB**
Bob Forcier, Pray Hill Rd, Box 475, RFD 2, Chepachet, RI 02814, U.S.A.

**DALLAS/FORT WORTH BASENJI CLUB**
Barbara Justus Smith, 3408 Pleasant Run Road, Irving, Texas 75062, U.S.A.

**THE BASENJI CLUB OF CINCINNATI**
Doris Kukuk Armbruster, 4579 Flowerstone Drive, Dayton, Ohio 45449, U.S.A.
Show Chairman: Rita L. Ross, 6226 Ridgewood Ct, Florence, KY 41042, U.S.A.

**COLORADO Hi-COUNTRY BASENJI CLUB**
Jo Ann Weller, 15580 East 144th, Brighton, Colorado 80601, U.S.A.

**BASENJI CLUB OF NORTHERN CALIFORNIA**
Margaret Sommer, 15091 Esther Drive, San Jose, California 95124, U.S.A.

**'THE SHOW-ME BASENJI CLUB'**
Pat Wood, 3500 West Terrace, Lea Wood, Kansas 66206, U.S.A.

**MAGNOLIA BASENJI CLUB**
Dorothy Brashear, 2700 Bayshore Boulevard, Dundein, Florida 33528, U.S.A.

**BASENJI CLUB OF SOUTHERN CALIFORNIA**
JoAnne W. Fimlaid, 14171 Elystan Cir, Westminster, California 92683, U.S.A.

**THE MAINELY BASENJI CLUB**
Gail K. MacLean, N. Raymond Road, Gray, Maine 04039, U.S.A.

**OBEDIENCE EXCHANGE U.S.A.**
Linda Benson, 3325 W. Palmer Street, Chicago, Illinois 60647, U.S.A.

**BASENJI HOUND CLUB OF NEW SOUTH WALES**
President: Alan Hunt, Derriwong Lane, Dural, NSW 2154, Australia.

**BASENJI CLUB OF VICTORIA**
Jan Bricknall, Scots Angle Road, Wattle Glen, Victoria 3096, Australia.

**BASENJI CLUB OF CANADA**
Anne Mander, 1513 Alexandra Blvd, Mississauga, Ontario L5E 2B5, Canada.

**SVENSKA BASENJISÄLLSKAPET (SBS)**
Chairman: Mia Lowbeer, Arkovagen 25-II, 121 55 Johanneshov, Sweden;
Secretary: Elisabeth Selinus, Valbovägen 4, 803 70 Gävle, Sweden

**BASENJI MAGAZINE U.S.A.**
Published monthly by Jon and Susan Coe, 789 Linton Hill Road, Newtown, Pennsylvania 18940, U.S.A.

## NOTES ABOUT THE AUTHOR

Mrs Anthony St. Erme Cardew has owned and bred animals almost all her life; dogs being by far her greatest favourites. She has owned and loved Basenjis since girlhood in the forties and knew personally some of the original imported dogs.

Apart from winning the highest awards in the Basenji Show Ring, Mrs St. Erme Cardew (or Mirrie, as she is known to her family and friends) has had the honour to judge Basenjis at 'Crufts' and is a well-known International Championship show judge of the breed. She has also had the pleasure of judging the American Basenji Club Speciality Championship Shows in Tulsa, Oklahoma and Buffalo; the Canadian Basenji Speciality in Winnipeg and the Victoria Basenji Championship Show in Melbourne (Australia).

Several top Basenji champions were bred or owned by Mrs St. Erme Cardew — many carrying the 'St. Erme' prefix and some going as puppies to pet homes, where they have later become Show Champions as well as much loved companions of their proud owners.

The author hopes the breed will never become commercialised but will remain the ideal companion and pet — being part of the family circle as he has for so many centuries: from the days where he sat around the cooking pot in his African straw hut to his basket by the Aga in 20th Century Britain.